PetCraft

PetCraft

100 Things Kids Can Make for Their Pets

Jackie Vermeer

NEW CENTURY PUBLISHERS, INC.

Printing Code
11   12   13   14   15   16
Library of Congress Cataloging in Publication Data
Vermeer, Jackie.
  Petcraft.
  Includes index.
  Summary: Provides illustrated instructions for
making toys, beds, and other gifts for your pet.
  1. Pet supplies—Juvenile literature.
2. Handicraft—Juvenile literature. [1. Pet
supplies. 2. Handicraft] I. Title.
SF413.5.V47   745.593   82-2287
ISBN 0-8329-0135-0   AACR2

To Kristi and David

Contents

Acknowledgments

To Mark Cochran, Jane and Chris Elswick, Stephanie Pemberton, John, David and Susie Shubert, and Kristi and David Vermeer, I express my gratitude for sharing their ideas, their pets and their enthusiasm. Thank you to Duane Davis for his excellent photography. And a most special thanks to my husband, Lou, and my children, Kristi and David, for all their help throughout the development of this book.

All drawings and illustrations are by the author.

All black and white and color photography by Duane D. Davis, except the photograph appearing on page 119, which is by Gayle Smalley.

PetCraft

1

Kittens and Cats

Kittens and cats are some of the most popular pets for youngsters. After all, who can resist a soft, cuddly, playful kitten? These animals are affectionate, adaptable, but at times independent, and their needs are few.

A Kitty Bed

Every kitten or cat needs a special place to sleep. They usually prefer an out of the way place which is soft and quiet. A large basket or box can serve as a good bed for a cat. Heavy-weight cardboard boxes, such as the type used for shipping apples, oranges or bananas, work very well. A portion of one side should be removed to provide a doorway. The box can then be decorated, and the young owner can make the bed as plain or fancy as he or she desires. Perhaps a few felt pen drawings on the outside are all that is needed.

A decorated kitty bed.

A more decorative look can be achieved by painting the outside with latex wall paint, and possibly adding wallpaper on the inside. Wallpaper sample books provide pieces large enough for one side. The same pattern, in different colors, can be used for the remaining sides.

After the decorating is completed, the bedding can be added. This can be most anything that is soft and washable. An old blanket or pillow, or even some of the child's outgrown shirts, can be tucked into a pillowcase to form the bedding. A few drawings on the pillowcase will make it extra special. Pictures of some of kitty's favorite things can be drawn on the pillowcase with permanent felt markers. Liquid embroidery also works well, and can be very colorful.

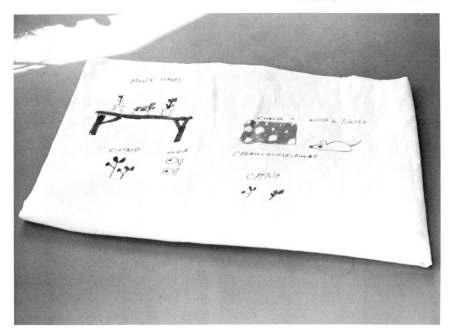

Kitty's own bedding cover.

Catnip Treats

A favorite treat for any kitten or cat is catnip. This plant is irresistible to cats. They love it—to eat, to roll in, or just to smell. A small patch of catnip planted in the garden is sure to be frequently visited. Perhaps the young cat owner would like to start his own private indoor garden. A plastic container, or the lower portion of a milk carton, can provide the necessary growing place. Add several inches of soil, plant the catnip seeds and water well. This planter should be covered with plastic wrap, or placed somewhere out of the cat's reach, otherwise the cat won't be able to wait for it to grow. When the plants are several inches high, the container can be placed near the kitty's bed for him to enjoy. Some of the catnip could be cut and dried for use in catnip toys.

Kitty enjoys his catnip garden.

Simple catnip toys can provide great fun for cats of all ages. A plastic egg-shaped stocking container makes an excellent toy. It makes a good rolling toy, but is an exceptionally good holder for catnip. For this use, choose a tight fitting container. First it will be necessary to make some small holes in the container, so the cat can smell the catnip. To do this requires a large needle, pushed into a cork and a lighted candle. Holding onto the cork, the end of the needle can be held in the candle flame for several seconds and then quickly pushed into the plastic. The hot needle melts the plastic, thus making a small hole. Make 6 or 8 holes in both the top and bottom portions of the container. All children should be well-supervised during this procedure, and reminded to hold onto the cork, not touching the needle, and of course to blow the candle out after all the

Personalized placemat.
(See pages 9 and 10.)

Kitty carrier.
(See pages 13–17.)

Dog backpack.
(See pages 25–28.)

Dog coat.
(See pages 28–30.)

Cage cover.
(See pages 38–41.)

Birds' Christmas tree.
(See pages 52 and 53.)

Milk carton birdhouse.
(See pages 55–58.)

Natural feeding place.
(See pages 41–43.)

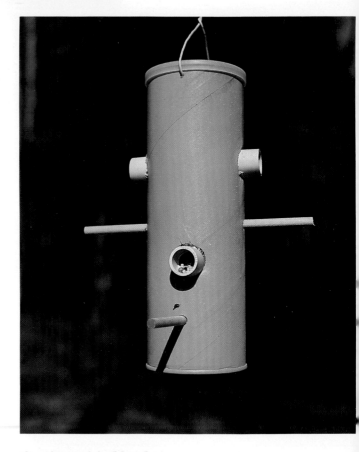

Canister birdfeeder.
(See pages 46–52.)

Small pet carrier.
(See pages 69–72.)

Milk carton insect house.
(See pages 83–85.)

Large size insect home.
(See pages 87–90.)

Rabbits are soft cuddly pets.
(See pages 91–94.)

Colorful bareback pad.
(See pages 98 and 99.)

Personalized water pail.
(See page 98.)

Colorful yarn animals.
(See pages 101–111.)

Super snake.
(See pages 104–106.)

Finger puppet and fuzzy lamb.
(See pages 116 and 117.)

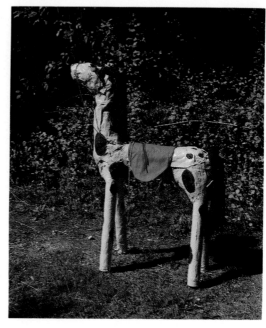

Colorful horse with saddle pad and stirrups.
(See pages 122–125.)

Heating the needle in the candle flame.
                    Making the holes in the container.

holes are made. Now, place approximately 1 teaspoon of fresh or dried catnip in the container and close it securely. Felt markers can be used to decorate the egg, if desired. Because of the egg-shape, the container will roll in various directions, and any cat would have great fun chasing this wonderful smelling toy. After several days, the catnip will lose its smell, then the container can be opened and a new supply placed inside.

Small fabric bags or felt animals can also be made to hold dried catnip. Small swatches of fabric can be stitched together to form a small packet into which a bit of catnip can be placed, and then stitched closed. For these small toys, it is a good idea to put the dry catnip in a fold of cotton before placing it in the toy. This will give the toy more padding thus making it easier for the cat to hold onto the

A catnip egg makes a great toy for a cat.

A variety of catnip toys.

toy. The felt mouse also contains cotton-wrapped catnip. For this toy, two shapes were cut from brightly colored felt, the catnip tucked in, and then the two sides were glued together.

Kitty Playthings

Kittens are especially playful, but even an older cat enjoys a toy now and then. Rolling toys, such as a ball of yarn or a ping pong ball, provide fun and exercise for cats of all ages. A spool toy can be a new kind of rolling toy. It can be easily made from two large thread spools, a length of yarn and two beads. Use a piece of yarn about 10 inches long, thread one bead onto the yarn and tie a knot at the end of the yarn so the bead will not slip off. Next, thread the two spools onto the yarn. If the yarn is heavy, a crochet hook

Kitty toys.

will simplify the threading. Then add the remaining bead
and knot the end of the yarn. The small beads prevent the
spools from slipping off the yarn.

The little yarn puff is an amusing plaything. It is light
enough so a cat can easily toss it about. It is simply made
by wrapping a length of yarn around a 1 inch wide piece
of cardboard. Tie the loops together tightly at one side of
the cardboard, and cut the loops on the opposite side.
Fluff the ends a bit, and it's ready. The child may even enjoy tossing it around a bit himself before giving it to his
kitty.

Cats of all ages love an empty bag or box. Curiosity will
get the best of them, and they may crawl inside, paw at it,
and even pounce on it. This will provide great entertainment for the cat and the audience as well.

Placemats

Maybe your youngster would like to brighten up kitty's eating corner. A special placemat can be a cheerful addition, and also helps keep the floor clean. A placemat can be very simple or quite elaborate. The easiest one to make requires a piece of butcher paper, construction paper or light-weight cardboard. The child can paint or draw a picture or design on the appropriate size paper or cardboard. When the picture is completed, the paper is covered on both sides with clear adhesive-backed plastic. Allow the plastic to overlap 1 inch on each side of the placemat so it can be sealed all the way around. The plastic covering makes the finished placemat permanent, and it can be easily cleaned with a damp cloth.

Kitty placemat using a paper background.

Placemat made of fabric, with iron-on tape design.

A similar kind of placemat can be made using fabric instead of the paper or cardboard. Here the design is made with iron-on tape. Before ironing the design in place, be sure that each piece has the adhesive side next to the fabric, otherwise it will stick to the bottom of the iron instead of the placemat. After the design has been ironed on, the placemat is then covered with the adhesive-backed plastic. It might be a good idea to have extra materials available, the youngster may wish to make a placemat for himself!

Building a Scratching Post

Every cat needs a scratching post and unless one is provided they will soon find their own place to scratch, such as the sofa, carpet or an upholstered chair. A few pieces of wood, some nails, and a carpet remnant are all that are required to make a scratching post. The base for the post should be large enough to prevent the post from tipping over easily. A piece of plywood 10 inches by 12 inches will provide a good base. Glue or nail a piece of carpeting onto

Scratching post.

Nailing the post and the base together.

Scratching posts can be fun for a cat.

the top of the plywood. To make the post, use two 18-inch lengths of 2-inch by 4-inch boards. Nail these boards together to form a 4-inch square post. Glue or nail carpeting around the post, and add a square to cover the top. Turn the post upside down, and place the base on top—with the carpet against the bottom of the post. Nail together. Turn right side up and put in a convenient place.

Collars

The simplest thing a child can make for his pet cat is a collar. A brightly colored ribbon tied around the kitty's neck can be very charming. For something a little more lasting, a length of fancy edging could be used, with nylon

Simple cat collars.

fasteners stitched to the ends to hold the collar together. Small, light weight, wooden beads can be strung to form an unusual collar. The important thing here, is making the collar the right size for the cat. If the collor is too small, the cat will be uncomfortable and if it is too big, his leg may get caught in it. A good rule of thumb when fitting a collar is to allow enough room for two fingers to easily slip into the collar along side the kitty's neck.

Traveling with Kitty

Some cats can be trained, with a little care and patience, to walk on a leash. For this, it may be a good idea to begin with a harness. A fairly sturdy harness can be constructed from grosgrain ribbon. First make a circle of ribbon large enough to fit over the cat's head, and stitch the ends together. Make a second circle large enough to go around the cat's waist, and stitch the ends together. Two more lengths of ribbon will be needed to connect the two circles together—one will go down the front between the legs, and the

Cat harness.

other down the cat's back. The lengths of these pieces will be determined by the size of the cat. First sew the front, or bottom, strip in place. Before sewing the back, or top, strip in place, slip a plastic curtain ring on the ribbon, this is for attaching a leash. After the stitching has been completed, slip the harness on the cat, and attach a leash. The leash itself can be another length of ribbon, or perhaps some colorful braided yarn. Now, off you go for a walk.

Traveling case.

There may be times when a cat needs to go on a short trip, perhaps to visit school with its owner, or to the veterinarian's office for its check up and vaccinations. These trips can be frightening to some pets—strange places, new faces and possibly other animals. For these special occasions the young owner may want to construct a traveling case for his cat. An orange or apple shipping box is perfect for this use. It is a double box made of heavy cardboard, with a small opening at each end for carrying.

To make the traveling case, separate the two parts of the box, and using the upper portion of the box, construct the case as follows:

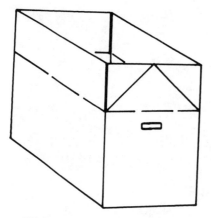

Figure 1

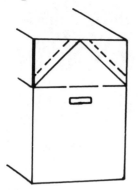

Figure 2

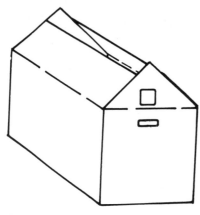

Figure 3

1. On the top of the lid, carefully lift open the flaps.

2. Measure across the end flap to find the center of the flap. Then draw lines from the center point to the bottom corners of the flap.

3. Bend the corners toward the inside along the lines.

4. Measure 1½″ from the fold, toward the corners, and cut as shown by the dotted lines in Figure 2.

5. Repeat this procedure with the other end flap.

6. If desired, small windows can be cut in the end flaps to provide additional ventilation, and a place for kitty to look out.

7. Apply glue to the folded edges of the end flaps, then fold the side flaps into place.

8. Cut an additional piece of cardboard, or poster board, to form the roof. It should overlap enough to allow a 1″ overhang on each side.

9. The box and the roof can now be painted and decorated, if desired. The youngster may wish to decorate the traveling case like a house, or car, or perhaps even a travel trailer.

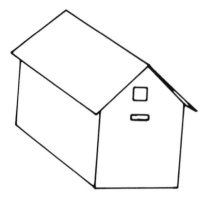

Figure 4

10. After painting, the roof can be glued in place and then should be allowed to dry thoroughly.

11. Slip the decorated top over the bottom portion of the box and it's ready to go.

Since the bottom portion of the box will serve as a temporary bed, some soft padding should be placed inside. It is a good idea to allow the cat a little time to become familiar with the traveling case—a nap or two, or some little trips around the house will help the cat to feel more at home in the case.

Happy traveling.

2

Puppies and Dogs

A puppy, or a dog, makes a wonderful pet for a youngster. Dogs are affectionate and intelligent animals. They can become a very special, and quite often protective, companion for a child.

Puppy's Bed

One of the first things a puppy needs is a bed. A sturdy cardboard box or wooden fruit crate works well. Remove the top, if there is one, and the front side. If a wooden crate is used, smooth any rough edges with sandpaper. Fill the bottom of the bed with soft material, such as a piece of blanket or towel. Some of the child's outgrown clothing makes a good padding under the blanket or towel, and also helps the puppy to become familiar with his new owner's scent. Some puppies will eventually outgrow their beds, and then can be encouraged to sleep on a larger blanket or rug.

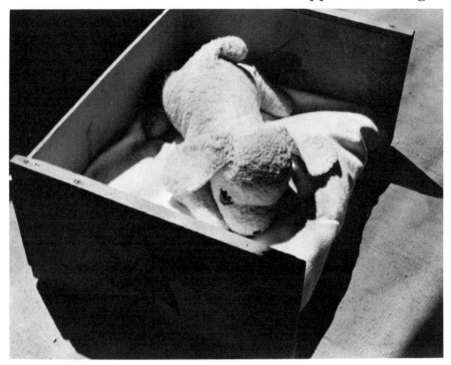

Star's bed. This bed, which has been outgrown by the puppy, now provides a resting place for a stuffed animal.

Puppy's Placemat

A placemat is a good project for a child to make for his dog. A placemat of the desired size can be cut from fabric and a design, or the dog's name, drawn on with felt markers. The fabric is then placed between sheets of adhesive-backed plastic. Allow an extra inch on each side so the plastic can be sealed all the way around to make it waterproof. Thus, any food or water which is spilled can easily be wiped up and the placemat can be used for a long time.

Another type of placemat can be made by weaving strips of colored construction paper or light-weight cardboard.

Max's placemat.

Cut the strips 2 inches wide and 24 inches in length. Place eight of these side by side to form the finished size of the placemat. Cut 12 additional strips 2 inches by 16 inches and begin weaving these through the first strips. Glue this first strip in place, and use paperclips to hold it securely while the glue dries and continue the weaving. After the weaving has been completed, glue along the outside edges, where the strips overlap. This placemat can also be sealed in adhesive-backed plastic to make it waterproof.

Woven placemat.

If the puppy or dog dish is plastic, it can be personalized with permanent felt markers. The printing will be fairly permanent and will last through quite a number of washings.

Things for Puppy to Chew

Children love to give their pets special treats to eat. Dog biscuits can be fun to make, and the dog or puppy will certainly enjoy them.

DOG BISCUITS

10 oz. beef broth
2 eggs
½ teaspoon baking powder
3 cups whole wheat flour
1 cup soy flour

½ cup wheat germ
½ cup vegetable oil

Place dry ingredients in a bowl, add remaining ingredients and mix well. Roll out on floured board to ¼ inch thickness. Cut with table knife or cookie cutters dipped in flour. Bake on lightly greased cookie sheet in 350°F oven for about 20 minutes or until the edges are lightly brown and the biscuits are firm. Cool thoroughly before feeding to pet.

Puppies are notorious for chewing up their owner's favorite shoes and slippers. When puppies begin to get their permanent teeth they need something to chew on, and it is a good idea to provide something for this purpose. Older dogs also enjoy chewing toys now and then. Reassure the puppy, or dog, that it is his toy and it's alright to chew it—with a firm "no" for anything else he may decide to try. There are many possibilities for chewing toys. Leather is good to chew, and is very lasting. An old leather belt, with the metal portions cut off, can be knotted at the ends to form a leather bone. The ideal chewing toy is a worn-out baseball glove. These can often be purchased, inexpensive-

Dog biscuits.

Chewing toys.

ly, at second-hand or thrift shops. The glove should, of course, be well-washed before giving it to the pet. An old clean sneaker, with the shoelace removed, is good. A soft rubber ball, or a used tennis ball, will provide additional exercise for a dog. They can chew it, toss it, chase it or even play a game with it.

Making a Collar

Perhaps your child would like to make a collar for his dog. Finger knitting is a quick method of making a collar.

Heavy yarn or roving is very good for this. First knot the yarn to a 1-inch plastic curtain ring. Form a loop of yarn near the ring, bring the rest of the yarn across the front and around to the back of the loop. Pull a loop of yarn through the first loop. Continue pulling loops through until the weaving reaches the desired length. Pull the end of the yarn through the last loop and pull tightly. Add another 1-inch plastic ring and tie securely. To form the collar, push a portion of the weaving through the ring and pull until the two rings come together. The collar can now be slipped over the dog's head. For a wider collar, two strands of yarn could be woven as a single strand.

Pulling the yarn through to form another loop.

Another type of decorative collar can be made from felt. Cut two strips of felt 1½ inches wide and the necessary length for the dog's neck. The two strips can be glued or stitched together, thus making a fairly sturdy collar. Colorful felt designs can be added to the outside of the collar if desired. Add nylon closures at each end for fastening.

The simplest collar for a large dog is a child's belt. It could be most any type of belt such as fabric, leather or plastic. Buckle it onto the dog's neck, making it just tight enough that it won't slip over his head easily.

Braiding a Leash

A braided leash could be constructed from a pair of 72-inch rawhide boot laces and an equal length of yarn. Holding the three strands together, form a loop at one end and knot. Then braid the three strands and knot again near the end. The loop can be slipped onto the belt collar before buckling, and then it's ready to go.

This dog wears a finger knit collar.

Making a Backpack

Often during the spring and summer, children like to take their dogs and go on a little hike or picnic. A dog backpack is just the thing for these occasions. They can take a sandwich and some dog biscuits, or other important provisions for their trip. To make a backpack, follow the directions given on pages 27 and 28, adjusting the measurements as necessary to fit your dog.

Other dog collars and a braided leash.

Dog backpack.

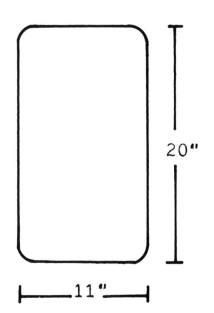

Figure 1

1. Cut a rectangle 20″ by 11″ from colored felt or fabric. Trim the corners. This piece will fit like a saddle over the dog's back.

Figure 2

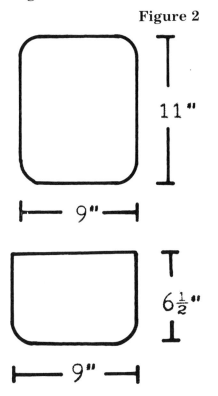

2. Make two pack bags, one for each side. Cut two pieces of each shape shown in Figure 2. The larger piece will form the back and the flap of the bag. The smaller piece will form the pocket of the bag.

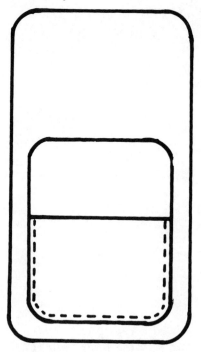

Figure 3

3. Position the two bag pieces on one side of the first piece. Stitch in place as shown by the dotted lines. Repeat on the other side.

Figure 4

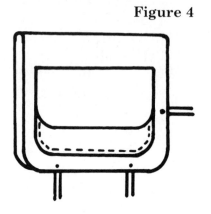

4. Position ties of bias tape on each side of the backpack and stitch in place. Two pair will tie under the dog's stomach and the front pair will tie across the chest—this will keep the pack from slipping backward.

Things to Wear

Staging a backyard circus or pet show can be great fun for children. They can spend hours planning for the grand production. A coat would be just the thing to

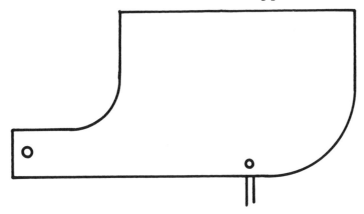

Coat pattern.

This dog has his coat on, ready for the show.

A dog's circus hat.

dress up a youngster's dog for the event. Felt or other fabric can be cut in the shape shown, according to your dog's size. The coat should overlap 2 inches at the chest, so a nylon closure can be used to help keep the coat in place. Ties attached, as shown, can be tied across the stomach.

A paper cone, tied in place with yarn, makes a funny dog hat for the show.

The Dog House

A dog house is always a good project for a youngster who especially enjoys working with wood. The type of wood pieces available will determine the kind of house to be built; however, a child usually has already decided exactly how he or she wants it to look. Children can do some pretty great building on their own, and if help is needed they'll ask, but no dog house will ever be better than that built "all by myself".

A-frame dog house.

3

Birds

Pet birds can be a great source of enjoyment to a child, as well as to the whole family. As pets, birds are quite easily maintained and offer great satisfaction. Some can be taught to imitate words, while others sing a lovely song.

Building a Cage

A bird's requirements consist primarily of a cage with food and water. The cage in the photograph on page 33 can be made with the help of an adult. A child can easily make the equipment and toys inside. Perhaps after making some things, he will invent some of his own.

To make the cage requires a 4-foot length of ½-inch mesh wire fencing, 36 inches wide. This size wire is often called rabbit wire because it is so often used in the construction of rabbit hutches. You will also need a 15-inch diameter oil

Constructed bird cage.

pan, available from an automotive department or store, some S-hooks, fine wire, and several ½-inch dowels. Bell or thermostat wire is very good for children to use. This is a plastic-coated fine copper wire that is very flexible and easy for children to work with.

To begin, overlap the cut ends of the wire fencing, so that it just fits inside the pan. Using 3- or 4-inch pieces of the bell wire, tie the fencing together at the seam. Using a large nail, hammer four holes in the sides of the pan near the top edge. Make the holes about the same distance

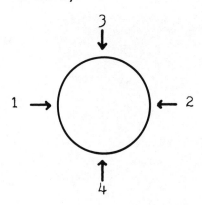

Make the holes in the order indicated, as an aid in proper spacing.

apart. To do this, make one hole, then make another hole on the opposite side of the pan. Make a third hole halfway between the first two, and then make the fourth hole opposite that. See the figure above. It is easiest to lay the side of the pan over the end of a sawhorse or workbench so as to have a firm surface under the pan. This will prevent denting the pan. After making the holes, it is a good idea to flatten the rough edges on the inside of the hole by pounding the hole with a hammer. Through each of the four holes attach a circle of wire. Use four S-hooks to attach the pan to the cage. You may wish to connect two of the wires directly to the cage, using the S-hooks to connect the remaining two wires. This will allow partial opening of the bottom for cleaning, rather than having the entire bottom removeable. Cut one 36-inch dowel into halves, then push these through the mesh near the top of the cage at right angles to each other. A large S-hook around the two dowels at the point where they meet will serve as a hanger. To add the top of the cage, cut out a circle of screen or cardboard to fit. The cage in the photograph has a piece of window screen cut to fit, with a slot for the hanger hook. The screen can be held in place with additional bell wire. This cage can then be hung from a ceiling hook, from a length of chain or perhaps even an attractive rope hanger.

The cage now needs a door. Cut out a rectangular section

Placement of dowels at the top of the cage for hanging.

of selected size, 4 inches by 5 inches is good. The cut out section may be used, or cut a new slightly larger piece for the door. The cut edges should be covered with a 1-inch wide adhesive cloth tape. This can be bandage, decorative or duct tape, all work equally well. Attach the door with wire hinges.

Now the cage is completed and the real fun begins. Add additional dowel sections for perches wherever desired by simply pushing the dowels through the wire mesh. Perhaps the young cage builder will want to add a swing made from a short length of dowel and suspended by fishing line or wire.

Cage Perches

An ideal perch is a small tree branch, trimmed to fit into the cage. The various size branches offer good exercise for the bird's feet. By wiring the branch to the side of the cage,

Various size perches are provided by using both dowels and a section of tree branch.

A hanging mirror provides amusement for a bird.

it will remain steady as the bird hops about on it and while the cage is being cleaned. Birdseed and water can be offered in spray can lids or other small plastic containers. Choose an appropriate size container, and perhaps decorate it with some flowers or designs using permanent felt pens. These also can be wired in place if desired. Cage birds enjoy fresh greens as part of their diet, and they would most certainly enjoy their own garden. Birdseed can be planted in small plastic containers or small flower pots.

Several containers, each planted a week apart, will assure a continuing supply of fresh greens.

Exercise Toys

Cage toys are important for additional exercise. A ping-pong ball is enjoyed by some birds. Small mirrors, such as from a ladies compact, are also fun for the bird. Glued to a piece of ribbon or yarn, they are a bright addition to any cage. A hanging bell can also be an interesting toy for the bird.

Any of the equipment or toys suggested can be easily adapted for use in a ready-made cage, if this is preferred.

Covering the Cage

Whether you make a cage or buy one, it should have a cover to be used at night. Birds, like some children, need to be reminded that it's time to rest, and covering the cage with a cloth will help ensure a rest period for the bird. Perhaps covering the cage could be part of the young owner's bedtime routine.

A cover can be made from a section of bed sheet. By using the upper portion of the sheet, the hemmed edge can be used to hold the tie. Cut open one end of the hem, and measure 54 inches across. This width is sufficient to go around the cage with enough to overlap at the edges. Measure down 48 inches from the hem. The child can stitch a hem at the bottom to give the cover a more finished look. The cage cover in the photograph has been decorated using liquid embroidery. This paint comes in a tube with a ball-point tip and is available in a wide range of colors. Using one of these tubes is much like drawing with a ball-point pen. Be sure to lay a piece of blotter paper under the fabric, as this gives a good drawing surface and protects the table from paint. After the paint has dried overnight, run a piece of yarn or ribbon through the upper hem and the cover is ready for use.

Cage cover.

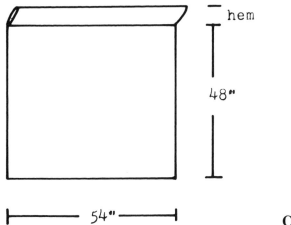

hem

48"

54"

Cage cover pattern.

A cheerful cover for a ready-made cage.

The previous photograph shows an example of a cover for a ready-made cage. To determine the size of fabric needed, measure up one side, across the top and down the opposite side. Then measure the front, top and back. Cut the fabric using the two measurements. The cage in the picture required a 36″ square of fabric. Cut a small slit in the center of the cloth for the handle or hanger and place the cloth over the cage. Trim away excess fabric at the corners, so that the edge of the cover comes to the bottom of the cage. This could be difficult for young children to cut evenly, in which case you may want to cut the first corner, remove the cover and let the child use the cut corner as a pattern to do the other three. The edge can be left as is, or as a finishing touch, trimmed with lace. Cut open one side all the way to the handle slit. This will make it possible to put the cover on without having to take down the cage. Add ribbon ties for closing. Here, the decorations have been made with colored iron-on tape. The designs are cut from various colors of tape and placed in position. Design details can be drawn with felt pens. Before the child irons on the design, check to see that all the pieces of the design have the adhesive side down, otherwise they will stick to the iron rather than the fabric. Remind the child to set the iron down on the design rather than pushing the iron across it. Many children have not had previous experience with iron-on tape, and need these little hints in order to avoid disappointment. After the design has been ironed on, allow the fabric to cool, and the cover is then ready for use.

Enjoying and Feeding Wild Birds

Attracting wild birds to a feeding station can provide many hours of enjoyment for the whole family. It is interesting to watch how many different kinds of birds come to feed and to attempt to identify each kind.

A feeding station can be set up at any time of year, but it is always busiest during the winter months when natural foods are not as plentiful. One of the surest methods of attracting birds is to hang a good-sized piece of suet. Ask for it at any meat counter or butcher shop. Place it inside a piece of plastic mesh and hang in a tree or under the eaves near a window. Onions are often sold in mesh bags, as are oranges and apples, and one small bag will provide enough mesh for several suet feeders. The mesh bag holder is especially good for a suet feeder, as the birds can hang onto the mesh while pecking at the suet.

Smaller pieces of suet can be melted in a pan over low heat, then the liquid can be poured into containers. After cooling, the fat solidifies again. Small cardboard containers can be used for the liquid fat, and after it has hardened the containers can be nailed to a small section of a tree

Mesh bag suet feeder.

branch. The branch provides a foot hold for the birds while feeding.

   Possibly your child would like to add something special to the melted fat, like some corn meal or peanut butter. In the photograph, jar lids were nailed to a piece of wood to provide containers for the special mixtures. This type of holder should be placed on a rock or table for feeding, as it has no perching place for the birds.

   Wild birdseed is readily available, and does not require

Log suet feeder.

a special feeder. It can simply be spread on a board, stump, table or porch for feeding.

Even a very young child can make this birdseed feeder. It is just a piece of plywood with a nail pounded through it—so that the nail comes out the other side. The nail is there to hold a special treat such as an apple, ear of corn, or maybe a piece of dry doughnut. The wild birdseed is scattered on the board and then it is set out. A tree stump could be used instead of the plywood—in which case a finishing

Jar lid feeders.

nail is pounded into the stump for the corn. You may also find the corn is irresistible to squirrels.

Some very simple hanging feeders can be made from a milk carton or a dried gourd. Use the bottom 1 inch of a milk carton. A 1-gallon size is very good, but smaller sizes also work well. Make a hole in the bottom at each corner. Tie an 18-inch piece of string through each corner and join them together. Tie to another string or a wire for hanging.

A gourd hanger will vary in size and shape depending on the type of gourd used. Use a large enough portion of the gourd to hold a supply of birdseed. Put a small hole in the bottom to allow any moisture to drain through. Make two or three holes around the edge to attach string hangers.

If your child likes to build things, this hanging feeder

Board feeder.

will be just the thing. Collecting scrap pieces of wood may be the only preparation necessary. The cover is slightly larger than the base to provide good protection for the birds from rain or snow. The side pieces do need to be the same length, and a little sawing may be necessary to assure this. The pieces can then be nailed together. An eye screw placed in the center of the roof can be attached to a wire for hanging.

To support a platform feeder, a sturdy stick (2 inches by 2 inches is good) can be pounded into the ground. Use a board about 16 inches by 8 inches for the platform, and nail onto the underside 2 blocks of wood to help steady the board. End pieces of 2 inch by 4 inch boards are perfect for this use. Find the center of the platform, lay the post across

Stump feeder.

the center, and position the small blocks. Mark the position of the blocks with a pencil or crayon. Then remove the post and blocks. Glue the blocks in place according to the marks, and when the glue is dry turn the board over and nail the blocks in place from the top. Glueing keeps the blocks in place, otherwise they are sure to move out of place. After the post is pounded into the ground, place the platform on the top and nail. Add the seeds and watch for visitors.

A tall foil-lined cardboard snack container can be turned into a very attractive hanging feeder. In addition to the canister, you will also need to provide two 7-inch lengths of ¼-inch diameter dowels and four 1-inch diameter plastic

Feeding platform.

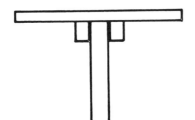

This diagram shows the placement of the blocks under the platform.

Hanging feeders.

pipe connectors. The youngster can paint the outside of the canister with enamel if he wishes. After the paint has dried, make four holes with a nail, for the dowel perches. These holes should be made in pairs. Make the first pair of holes 1½ inches from the bottom of the canister, on opposite sides as shown in the following diagram. Then make a second pair of holes 4½ inches from the bottom of the canister, on opposite sides and position the holes on the front and back of the canister. Two more pairs of holes will need to be made to hold the pipe connectors. Each of these four holes should be placed 1½ inches above each perch. It is easiest to make the holes first with a large nail, and then widen them by twisting the nose of a pair of pliers inward

Covered hanging feeder.

until the hole is large enough to hold the pipe connector tightly. Insert the four pipe connectors, and then push a dowel through each pair of small holes, for the perches. Add a piece of wire or string through the top of the canister, below the lid, for hanging. Fill the canister with birdseed. It is best to place the canister in a bowl while filling, to catch the seeds that slip out the feeding holes before it is filled.

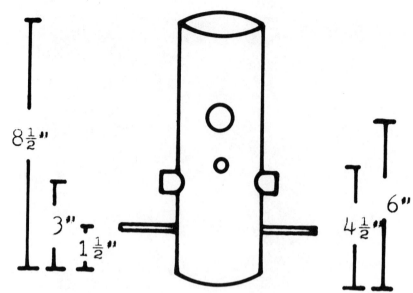

Measurements for constructing a canister feeder.

To attract the birds, hang this feeder near a suet bag, and while pecking at the suet, the birds will soon spy the seeds in the feeding holes. Then the fun begins.

Some birds find sunflower seeds especially delightful. There are two feeders that children can assemble to hold these treats. One feeder requires a 3-pound coffee can lid, a 5 inch by 12 inch section of ½-inch mesh wire fencing, the bottom of a one gallon plastic bleach bottle and a length of heavy wire for hanging. First remove the bottom portion of the clean bleach bottle, about 1½ inches deep. This plastic is fairly easy to cut with scissors. Make a hole in the center of the bottom for the wire. Push the wire through the hole and bend it over to hold the bottom in place—if using wire which bends easily, it can be wound around a small section of twig or dowel to support the feeder. Form the fencing into a cylinder and wire the ends together. Slip this over the wire and position it in the center of the feeder bottom. Fill this cylinder with sunflower seeds. Make a hole in the

Canister feeder.

center of the coffee can lid and slip the lid onto the wire. It is now ready to hang. Birds can easily peck the seeds out through the mesh.

A similar holder can be made using two 3-pound coffee can lids, a plastic berry basket and a piece of wire for hanging. Make holes in the centers of both lids. String the wire through one lid, and then the berry basket. Fill the basket with sunflower seeds and add the other lid.

Maybe your child would enjoy growing sunflowers in a

Sunflower seed feeders.

summer garden. Allow the flowers to completely develop, and the seeds will form in the center of the flower. The entire flower head can be saved and put out in the winter, and the birds can serve themselves.

The Christmas tree which provided enjoyment for the family during the holiday season can be used to provide more enjoyment by becoming a feeding tree for the birds. Any evergreen tree already growing in your yard would also work as well. Decorate the tree with all sorts of treats for the birds. Pinecones with bits of suet tucked in between the petals, apple slices, bits of bread spread with peanut butter, some raisins strung on a wire ring, or even strings of popcorn and cranberries—all delightful tidbits for visiting birds. The obvious advantage of the tree is that the

Christmas tree feeder.

branches provide good perches while eating or just a nice place to sit while watching you.

In early spring when the summer birds begin returning, it is time to think of providing places for them to nest. Some birds, particularly robins, prefer nesting platforms to regular closed bird houses. One can be easily constructed from wood scraps. The platform itself should be about 8 inches square. The roof should be at least an inch larger in each direction, to provide protection from rain. The platform requires a backboard 8 inches wide and approximately 14 inches long. A small block of wood is also needed to support and steady the platform. First the child should nail the platform onto the wood block. Then nail the block onto the backboard. Last of all, nail the roof on. It is then ready to be nailed up in a nearby tree. It should be high enough that summer leaves will shade it and provide it with some privacy.

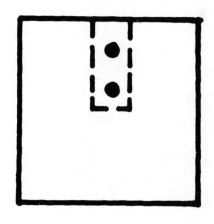

Nailing the platform to the block.

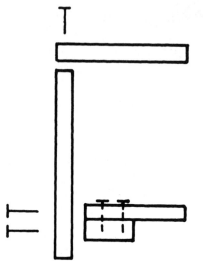

Nailing all the pieces together.

This nesting platform is all ready for a visiting robin.

Constructing a Birdhouse

A simple birdhouse can be made from a 1-gallon milk carton. Wash it out well, then measure up 4 inches from the bottom and make one hole on each side of the front, then matching holes on the back side. They should be large enough for a ¼-inch diameter dowel. To make the front door, measure up from the bottom 5½ inches and over 2¾ inches from one side. Make a circle 1⅛-inches in diameter

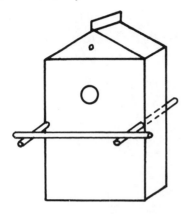

Placement of the dowels.

Milk carton birdhouse.

Nesting material.

and cut out. Make several holes in the bottom of the carton and also one inside the top front and top back (inside the fold area so it won't allow rain to get in). Staple the carton closed at the top and it is ready for painting. To finish the birdhouse, slip a 9-inch-long ¼-inch diameter dowel through from the front to the back, one on each side. Glue an additional piece across the two ends to form a front door perch. The perch should be about 2 inches from the carton. Using a wire for a hanger, attach it to the handle of the carton and hang the house in a tree where it will not be exposed to direct afternoon sun.

Your child may wish to supply some nesting material for the birds. A plastic mesh bag, like the suet bag, can be filled with soft lint from the clothes dryer filter, and bits of brightly colored yarn. Let the ends of the yarn hang out from the sack so the birds can easily pick it up.

Hummingbird Feeders

If hummingbirds visit your area during the spring or summer, a feeder for these birds will allow a glimpse of these fascinating creatures. These tiny birds require a different type of feeder and nectar instead of bird seed.

To construct a feeder will require a pint-size canning jar

Hummingbird feeder.

and a round watering tray. These watering trays are made primarily for watering chickens. They are made to be used with regular canning jars and thus have a threaded cap permanently attached to the inside of the tray, with small vents to allow the tray to remain filled with water. It will be necessary to pound four holes in the edge of the tray lip for attaching cord for a hanger.

The jar will need to be filled with nectar for the birds to drink. To make some nectar, heat 2 cups of water and ½ cup of sugar. Heat and stir until all the sugar has dissolved, then add a few drops of food coloring. Cool to room temperature before filling the feeder jar. Fill the jar, twist on the tray and, holding over the sink, turn the jar upside down. The tray will then partially fill with the liquid.

To attract the birds, some brightly colored flowers are needed. Using a bright colored construction paper cut several flower shapes about 1½ inches in diameter. Punch a hole in the center of each flower, with a paper punch, and insert a 2-inch section of a plastic drinking straw. Set the straws in the liquid in the tray. Hang the feeder out of doors and watch for visitors.

During the summer months, your child may also wish to set out small trays of water and watch the birds splash about taking a bath.

Now, happy bird watching all year long.

4

Small Cage Pets

If your youngster is fortunate enough to become the proud owner of a small cage animal, he is in for a great deal of enjoyment. Small animals such as gerbils, mice, rats, hamsters or guinea pigs are a furry handful. All of these little pets are affectionate, love attention and can be taught to do tricks. All the animals mentioned, with the exception of the guinea pig, act in a similar manner. They are gnawing animals, so they should be housed in a metal screen cage. Provide dry food, fresh water, a small salt block and occasional fresh vegetables. All the little animals particularly enjoy fresh hay—if that is available.

Building a Cage

A metal cage can be constructed from ½-inch mesh fencing (rabbit wire). A piece of screen 36 inches by 42 inches is

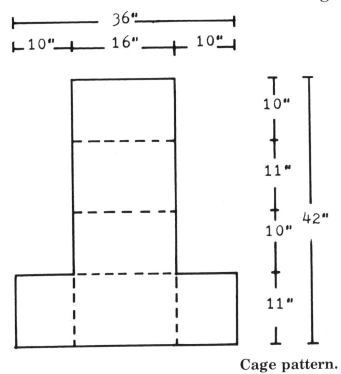

Cage pattern.

sufficient for a small animal. When the cage has been constructed, it can be placed in an 11-inch by 17-inch jelly roll pan or cookie sheet with low sides. The pan can hold kitty litter, newspaper or commercially prepared small animal litter. This makes cleaning the cage a very simple process. Lift out the cage, empty the pan, replace with fresh litter material, and replace the cage.

To construct the cage, cut the fencing according to the pattern above.

Fold the fencing according to the dotted lines in the diagram. Using a pliers, bend the sharp edges of the mesh over to connect the two sides. Close all sides and make sure no sharp edges protrude anywhere. In the front side of the cage, cut open a space for the door. Using the cut out section, or a new one, attach the door with wire hinges. Cover

Small animal cage.

the cut edges with 1-inch wide adhesive tape. The measurements for the cage could be altered to fit most any size pan.

Exercise Equipment

Any small animal needs some exercise, and it is a good idea to provide some kind of equipment in the cage for this. All animals, except guinea pigs, will use cage exercise equipment and toys. An exercise wheel can be constructed from a round salt box. Tape the spout closed, and paint the outside using a nontoxic paint. Glue on eight popsicle sticks around the outside of the box, then poke a dowel through the ends of the box. Make the dowel long enough

Exercise wheel.

to reach from one side of the cage to the other. You may wish to glue a small thread spool on each end of the dowel, on the outside of the cage, to keep it from slipping out of place.

A teeter totter can be made from the bottom of a cheese box. Push a dowel through the sides of the box. The dowels should be long enough to reach between the sides of the cage. To provide a change of activity for the pet, the teeter totter and the exercise wheel could be used alternately.

Teeter totter.

Building a Playpen

Maybe your youngster would like to make a playpen for his small animal. The one shown in the following photograph is made from particle board, cardboard and a disposable roasting pan. Three walls and a floor are made from the particle board to enclose a disposable pan. A cardboard shelf is made, to provide an upstairs, and glued in place.

Small animal playpen.

Part of the cardboard is cut and bent downward, with small pieces of dowel glued on, to provide stairs for the animal to scurry up and down. Provide toys such as a tissue tube to crawl through and a small table made from a wooden spool and a plastic lid glued together to climb on. A ping-pong ball is fun for the animal to push around and a hard-shelled nut is good for him to gnaw on to keep his teeth in good condition. A small mirror glued to the wall can also be an interesting addition.

This playpen could be a permanent home if a wire screen front and roof were added. Be sure to use wood on the sides, even though you may be tempted to substitute cardboard; small animals will chew through anything else. If this is to be a permanent home, provide a kind of bed for the animal.

Cocoa can will serve as a nesting place for this hamster.

Here a cocoa can, washed and painted, has been placed on the shelf for the animal to build its little nest in.

Caring for Guinea Pigs

Guinea pigs are the largest animals in this group but they are the least active, and the least intelligent. These are treated as a separate group because they are the simplest to care for and have the fewest requirements. They do not need exercise equipment, but they do like a little room to move around. Here a guinea pig is in a fairly large pen. The sides of the pen are 8-inches high, so the guinea pig will not get out as they do not climb or jump. The pen does not need to be covered unless there are other animals in the home which might hurt the guinea pig.

Guinea pig pen.

Provide a small box or a covering at one end of the pen so that the guinea pig will have a place in which to hide. These animals love fresh hay and fresh vegetables such as carrots, celery, lettuce, and apples in addition to their dry food. Clean straw makes excellent bedding for these animals, but if this is not available small animal litter can also be used. The youngster may wish to keep his guinea pig in a cage at night and then in the pen during the day. These small furry creatures learn to recognize their own-

ers, and love attention. They may squeal if they feel ig-
nored, or if they want a treat of fresh vegetables.

Creating a Maze

A maze can provide entertainment for the owner as well
as for the small animal. A large cardboard carton can be
used to form a maze, and it can be made in any size. A large
carton from a washer, dryer, or refrigerator is ideal. Lay

Maze.

the box on its side, and cut it so that the walls of the maze are about 6 inches high. Cut additional lengths of cardboard to provide walls inside the maze. Make doorways in the walls before gluing in place. Crosswalls can be held in place with masking tape, and then can be moved about later to change the maze pattern. A section of a paper towel tube will serve as a tunnel between different rooms. This tunnel provides a natural place to add a bridge. Fold a piece of cardboard to form the bridge and pieces of popsicle sticks can be glued in place for steps on the bridge. Place a small treat in one of the rooms, and time the animal to see how long it takes him to find the food. Repeat, with the food in the same place and see if the animal can make the trip in a faster time. It may be possible to have the animal learn several different patterns to the reward.

Small Animal Transport

Animals enjoy exploring your house, but it can be dangerous to allow them to run loose. By making a rolling pen,

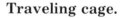

Traveling cage.

Carrying case for small animals.

the animal can explore and yet is safe from other animals and from getting lost.

Use a large size (9 ounce) snack canister. Cut away the center section of the canister leaving only about 1 inch at either end. Use a 14-inch by 10-inch piece of ½-inch wire mesh for the center portion of the traveling cage. Cover all the cut edges of the wire mesh with adhesive-backed tape. Roll the wire mesh into a cylinder and set into the bottom end of the canister. Slip the top ring of the canister over the other end of the cylinder, close the end with the resealable plastic lid and lay the container on the floor. As the animal walks the cage rolls, and he will soon learn to get around very well. This is good exercise and he will enjoy a short period in this traveling cage each day.

Quite often when a youngster goes on a walk or a short trip, he would enjoy taking his pet along. A plastic cottage cheese carton provides a good temporary carrying case. Put extra litter or tissues in the carton for bedding for the animal. Slip the carton inside a plastic mesh bag, such as an apple or onion bag. Run a string through the top to be able to tie it closed. It can be carried or the child could tie it to his belt. For some animals, it is best to have the cottage cheese carton lid for the top of the container. Occasionally

Coffee can carrier.

a small pet, particularly gerbils, will want to chew their way out of anything, and the lid, with several holes made for ventilation, will discourage this.

A 3-pound coffee can is easily converted to a carrying case for a larger animal, such as a guinea pig. Two holes can be made, on opposite sides of the can near the top, for attaching a wire handle. Make a number of small holes in the lid for ventilation. Some bedding should be placed in the bottom, and perhaps a piece of lettuce or carrot, before putting the animal inside.

5

Fish and Reptiles

Fish are good pets for children; they require a minimum amount of care while providing a fascinating show. Children love to sit and watch the fish darting through the water chasing each other and poking their noses into every plant and corner.

Maintaining the Goldfish Bowl

Goldfish can be maintained in a large bowl providing that the water is changed frequently. The fresh water should always be allowed to stand at least 24 hours so it will be the same temperature as that in the fish bowl. The youngster needs to be cautioned not to overfeed the fish, as overfeeding will make the water unsuitable for the fish. The bowl should also contain a layer of gravel on the bottom and some aquarium plants. The houseplant, Creeping Jennie or Moneywort, can be used in the aquarium. Simply

Goldfish live in a large glass bowl.

snip off several pieces of the plant and anchor them in the gravel or allow some to float on the surface. The plant will add oxygen to the water as well as provide the fish with hiding places.

The Aquarium

An aquarium makes a most suitable home for fish. Goldfish or tropical fish can live happily in a well-maintained aquarium for years. If your child chooses fish for pets, there are many colorful species of tropical fish which are sure to delight him. Your aquarium dealer can best advise you as to compatible types of fish and the proper number of fish for your particular aquarium size.

An aquarium does require a filter system, some gravel

A mural adds interest to an aquarium scene.

for the bottom and water plants. A few pretty rocks or marbles can also be placed in the bottom for decoration. Perhaps the child would like to draw an underwater mural for the back of his fish tank. The picture can be drawn using crayons, water colors, or felt pens. When the drawing is completed, tape it to the outside of the back of the tank.

Aquarium Toys

There are several aquarium toys which a child can make for his pet fish to enjoy. A series of rings or an arch for the fish to swim through are simple to make. The arch is made from sections of two bendable plastic drinking straws. Cut off about 2 inches of the bottom of each straw, then bend the two upper sections in the flexible area and join the tops together. The top of one straw is inserted into the top of the other straw. To do this one of the straws may need to be stretched a bit. This can be done by pushing the end of a ball-point pen a little ways into the straw end. Stretch until it will accommodate the end of the other straw. Now the arch is ready to be placed in the tank. Turn it upside down in the tank to fill the straws with water, then turn right side up and plant in the sand.

The connected rings shown in the photograph below were constructed from plastic air tubing. This tubing is usually available wherever aquarium supplies are sold. Each ring requires a 12-inch length of tubing. Make one or more of the rings by forming a circle of the tubing and slip one end inside the other. Again, it may be necessary to

Tank toys.

Tadpole aquarium.

stretch one of the ends a bit before it will accommodate the other end. The rings can be linked together or colored, by partially filling with colored water, before closing the ends.

Tadpole Aquarium

An aquarium makes an ideal home for keeping tadpoles. It is fascinating for youngsters to watch the growth and development of the tadpoles into frogs or toads. When collecting tadpoles, be sure to collect a good quantity of the pond water and also some of the natural food supply. Scrape a little sediment from the pond bottom and also some of the water plants growing there—these will provide the food for the tadpoles. As the water in the aquarium evaporates, it will be necessary to add fresh water to maintain an adequate water level for the tadpoles' activity. A rock, which reaches above the water line, will be necessary for the tadpoles after they have developed legs. After the tadpoles have changed into frogs or toads, you will want to return them to their pond so they can continue to grow properly.

Frog Terrarium

A small frog or toad can be housed in a terrarium with a screen cover. Moss, plants, a small water pool and a hiding place, such as a small piece of wood, are all necessary parts of a terrarium for this purpose.

The water should always be fresh and clean, and a fairly constant supply of flies and bugs is needed for food. Frogs

Terrarium home for a tiny tree frog.

and toads are very quick at catching live food and this is great fun to watch. After a time, it is desirable to return the frog or toad to its natural habitat.

Caring for Turtles

Turtles or tortoises also make most interesting temporary pets. They are, of course, easily caught and quite easy to care for. The first step is to identify the turtle or tortoise so that its food and environmental needs are met. As with most reptiles and amphibians, the skin is the first clue in identification of the animal. Slick, moist skin usually indicates a water lover—frogs, salamanders and turtles are in

An unused rabbit hutch provides a good cage for this pond turtle.

this group. A dry, scaly skin means it is primarily a land dweller—toads, lizards and tortoises belong to this group. Both groups need water for drinking, but the first group requires water for swimming, and some turtles will only feed in water.

Turtles need a pond or pool of water in which to swim, a board or log to crawl under for a place to hide and soil to burrow in. Plants and moss help make the environment seem more natural. Possibly a child's small plastic swimming pool could be used for a turtle home. A cage or wooden enclosure will also work, just be sure the turtle has plenty of room to move around. For a tortoise a large cardboard box can be used with a small pan or tray of water for drinking. Both turtles and tortoises enjoy fresh vegetables and bits of fruit to eat. After a time these animals, too, should be returned to the area in which they were found.

Studying the Snake

Perhaps the most temporary pet a child might bring home would be a snake. It may be temporary because of the difficulty of providing it with food. Some small snakes will do well with a good supply of insects; however, most snakes feed primarily on small rodents. Here, again, identification is important for proper feeding and housing. An unused aquarium is ideal for a small snake. Cover the bottom of the aquarium with sand and then dirt. Provide a small tray of water, a log or flat piece of wood for a hiding place and an area of grass and small plants. Some snakes like to climb, so a short branch might be a good addition to a snake's home. It is always a good idea to cover the aquarium with a screen to prevent the snake from escaping. Don't place the aquarium in full sunlight, as it will become too warm for the snake.

Snakes are fascinating creatures to watch, and your child may wish to keep one for several days before returning it to its original area.

Snake home.

6

Insects

Children have a natural curiosity about bugs, butterflies and other members of the insect world. These little creatures are easily caught and are most interesting to watch. First, of course, the insect needs to be caught, and either a butterfly net or collecting jar will be needed.

The Butterfly Net and Collecting Jar

The butterfly net is made from a 24-inch by 18-inch piece of nylon net, a wire coat hanger and a ½-inch diameter dowel. Fold the net in half and stitch the sides closed, making a pocket 18 inches wide and 12 inches deep. Pull on the bottom of a wire coat hanger until it forms a square shape. Now, wrap the open edge of the net around the coat hanger wire and stitch together. Straighten the hook end of the hanger and attach it to one end of the dowel with masking tape. It is now ready to capture flying insects.

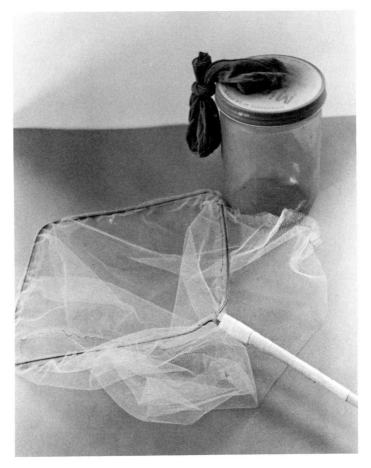

Butterfly net and collecting jar.

The collecting jar can be most any kind of wide mouth jar placed inside a nylon stocking. This is particularly good for young children, for if the glass jar breaks the stocking containing the broken pieces can be thrown away without the danger of cut fingers.

Insect Homes

There are a variety of insect homes which children can easily construct. A very simple one can be made from two

Screen insect cage.

disposable pie pans and a section of window screen. This
cage is particularly good for caterpillars or butterflies. One
pie pan serves as the cage bottom, and is partially filled
with damp soil or sand. Then shape the screen into a cylinder and staple together. Place the cylinder in the pie pan.
Small sections of plants can be placed in the sand to help
keep them fresh. Every caterpillar has a favorite kind of
plant on which it feeds, so it is wise to have children pick
some stems or branches from the plant on which the cater-

pillar is found. A fresh supply of food will be needed daily until the caterpillar has completed this growth stage and begins to spin his chrysalis or cocoon. For a butterfly provide flowers from which it can sip nectar. These flowers, too, will stay fresh longer if poked into the damp soil in the bottom. After the plant material has been placed in the soil or sand add the caterpillar or butterfly, and slip the second pie pan on top. This cage offers a good opportunity for viewing and plenty of fresh air.

Milk carton insect cage.

A milk carton can become another home for a caterpillar. Remove sections from two sides of the milk carton, paint if desired, and cover the openings with nylon net which can be glued to the carton. A small spray can lid, filled with soil or sand, can be used to hold the necessary plant material. After the caterpillar has been placed inside, close the carton top and fasten with a brad. It can be reopened as necessary to add a fresh food supply for the ever-hungry caterpillar.

Viewing box.

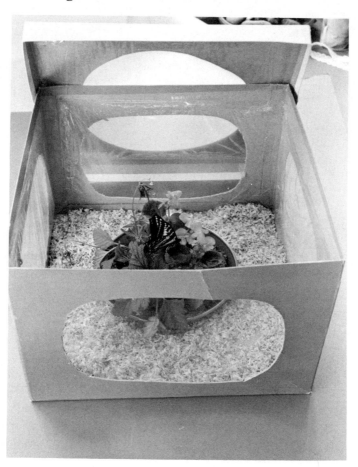

Looking in through the side window of the viewing box.

A viewing box is particularly good for butterflies and dragonflies as it provides more room for flying. A large gift box is ideal for this use. Large viewing holes are cut in each side and in the lid. These holes are then covered with plastic wrap, taped in place on the inside of the box. The bottom of the box can be covered with a layer of small animal litter, or sawdust. Place a plastic flower pot saucer, or similar container, in the center. The saucer could contain little plants and perhaps some flowers.

One type of cage that is adaptable for a variety of insects requires a 1-gallon plastic bleach bottle. Wash the bottle well before allowing a child to work on it. Remove about two-thirds of the side for a viewing place. Place sand, plants and insect in the bottle and tape a section of screen or net over the cut out area. If this is to be

Bleach bottle insect home.

used for small crawling insects, you may wish to place cotton balls inside the ends of the handle openings to prevent the insects from hiding in there and disappointing the viewer.

Glass jars also make good insect homes for small bugs and beetles. A glass canister provides a large opening for arranging the interior of the jar. A piece of nylon netting over the end, held in place with a string or rubber band allows ventilation. It is advisable to try to make a home similar to the place in which the insect was found. In the glass canister, the millipede's home is made up of moss, rocks, plants, a piece of decayed wood, and, of course, a small pool of water. Because the jar is round a stand has been constructed to keep it from rolling. The bottom por-

Glass canister is a home for a millipede.

A beetle lives inside this canning jar.

tion of a 1-gallon milk carton, with sides cut in a curve to fit the jar, makes a sturdy stand.

The canning jar in the photograph is furnished with small plants and moss and houses a little beetle. Because the jar is square in shape, it does not require a stand.

A lid can be used to prevent the insect from escaping, but it should be removed occasionally to prevent an excess buildup of moisture, and to provide ventilation.

It is always a good idea to try to identify an insect, in order to learn of any special requirements it may have and to find out what it eats. As with any wild creature, after observing it for awhile, return it to its natural home.

7

Outdoor Pets

There are a number of other animals which make very good pets, but are generally kept out of doors.

Rabbits as Pets

Rabbits, although they can live indoors, are most generally thought of as outdoor animals. These soft furry creatures can become quite tame and affectionate. Their diet should consist of commercial rabbit pellets and fresh vegetable greens. Fresh drinking water should always be available, as well as a spool of salt. One thing a child might wish to make for his pet rabbit is a name tag. A section of plastic, cut from a colored coffee can lid, can be fastened with wire to the front of the rabbit hutch. The name can be printed on the plastic tag with permanent felt markers.

A name tag identifies this rabbit.

Constructing a Rabbit Nesting Box

A female rabbit may need a nesting box in which to build a nest for her babies; however, all rabbits can use a similar box during the winter for protection from the cold weather. The necessary pieces for the box can be cut by an adult but a child can easily nail the box together. To make the box will require two pieces of wood 18 inches long and 13½ inches wide for the sides, two pieces 18 inches long and 11½ inches wide for the top and bottom. Nail these four pieces together, overlapping one edge of each side as shown in the diagram. The two end pieces should be 14 inches by 12 inches. One end piece should have an opening, at least

A snug and cosy nesting box offers protection from the weather.

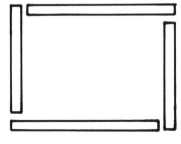

Nailing the sides of the nesting box together.

5½ inches high and 5 inches wide, cut in it for a doorway. After the end pieces have been nailed in place the box could be painted. A nice layer of straw or shredded newspaper should be placed inside for comfort and warmth.

Goats as Pets

A young goat makes a lively, and most interesting, pet. These, of course, need to be kept in an outdoor pen, and are

A baby goat wears a clover chain necklace.

Beginning a clover blossom chain.

certain to be a constant source of amusement to a child. A young goat could wear a dog collar, but a clover chain is more fun to make for this pet. To form the chain, make a small hole in the stem of a clover blossom, insert a second stem and make a small hole in its stem for the next stem. The chain can be made in any length desired, and to finish slip the first blossom through the hole in the last stem. This method works equally well with dandelions and other wild flowers. When the flower chain is completed, slip it over the goat's head quickly—or he may eat it.

A daisy chain is made in a different manner, and results in a heavier chain than the previous one. Take two or three daisies to start the chain, then wrap another daisy around the first ones. Continue this until the desired length is achieved, then holding the ends of the chain side by side add several more daisies tucking in the ends as they are wrapped onto the chain.

To add another flower, lay it under the chain.
Wrap the stem over the chain and around behind the
blossom.

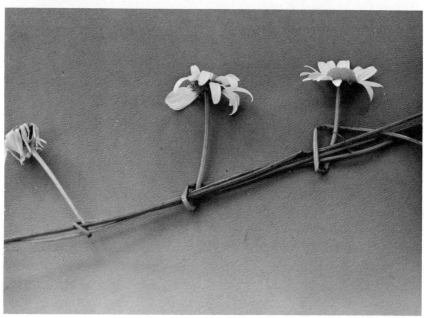

A daisy chain decorates this pony.

Caring for a Pony or Horse

Any youngster who has a pony or horse also needs some grooming aids to care for the animal. Brushes, a comb and a hoof pick are a few necessities. Perhaps a board on which to hang these implements is just the thing to keep them from being misplaced. A piece of plywood or particle board, about 12 inches by 18 inches, will serve as the background, with small finishing nails appropriately placed

Horse care board.

to hold the grooming aids. The board and the brushes will need small eye screws added to aid in hanging. The board can be painted and decorated however the child wishes.

A special washing or watering pail could be personalized. Paint the name, or a design, on the pail using enamel or other waterproof paint.

A bareback pad is a good project for a youngster who enjoys riding bareback. This pad makes the ride a little

Bareback pad.

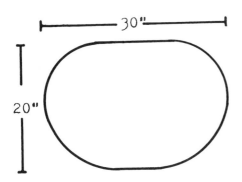

Bareback pad pattern.

softer and also protects the child's clothing from the dust in the horse's coat. Cut the bareback pad according to the above pattern. Use a heavy fabric such as felt or a quilted material. The edges can be turned under, or covered with fabric trim or bias tape.

A shaggy burro stands patiently while an old hat, with holes cut for his ears, is put on.

8

Created Pets

Sometimes a child's most favorite pet is the one that comes from his own imagination. He can make it big or small, happy or fierce, in any color he desires. No matter how it looks, it is always there waiting to be talked to and loved.

Pets Made with Yarn

Yarn can be used to make all sorts of pets. A yarn doll will easily slip into a small pocket to accompany its owner wherever he or she goes.

To make the doll's body, take a 5 inch by 2 inch piece of cardboard or poster board and wrap yarn around the length of the cardboard 20 times. Using a small piece of yarn or string tightly tie the yarn loops together at one end of the cardboard. Slip all the loops off the cardboard and, using another small piece of yarn, tie all the loops together about 1 inch from the first tie—this will form the head. The next

Yarn dolls.

step is to make the arms. Use a smaller piece of cardboard, about 4 inches long, and wrap the yarn around the length of it 10 times. Carefully slip the loops off the cardboard and tie them together about ½ inch from each end. Take the arm section and place it between the body loops, so that about half the strands go in front of the arms and the rest go in back of the arms. Slide the arms into position just below the head, and tie the body section in the middle to form the waist. For a girl doll, cut the body loops at the bottom to form a skirt. To make the doll a boy, divide the loops and tie each half about ½ inch from the bottom to form the legs and feet.

Little eyes or felt dots could be glued on for facial features, or even a few pieces of yarn hair for added character. These dolls can be made in most any size, but if they are made larger wrap the yarn more times to give additional fullness.

Yarn horse and a braided snake.

A playful yarn horse can be made in much the same way. Use at least an 8-inch length of cardboard, and make all three sections the same size. Make the two leg sections in the same manner as the arms of the doll, simply tying the yarn loops about ½ inch from each end. For the body, tie at one end of the cardboard, slip off the loops, and tie off about 1 inch for the head. Allow 2 inches for the neck, tie and then slip in one leg section, tie again before slipping in the other leg section. Tie again and cut the loops at the end of the body section to form the tail. This yarn horse is soft and cuddly, but needs a little help to stand up. Insert a pipe cleaner through each leg section and bend to shape the legs. An additional piece of pipe cleaner can be placed inside the neck section to hold up the head. Felt ears and a mane could be added if desired.

By using three different colors of yarn, a brightly colored braided snake can be created. Each snake requires three

Colored yarns form a snake and an octopus.

strands of yarn 2 feet long, in each of the three chosen colors. Take all nine strands and tie a large knot at one end to form the snake's head, the small loose ends can be the snake's many-forked tongue. Using a felt marker, draw two eyes on the snake's head. Separate the yarn strands according to color, and braid using the three strands of each color as a single strand. Use a small piece of yarn to tie the braid at the tail end. Now it is ready to curl up in the youngster's pocket.

A larger snake can be more fun to play with, but won't fit in a pocket as well. For this snake your child will need 21 strands of yarn, each 4 feet long. He may choose to have all the yarn the same color or a variety of colors. Take all the strands together and fold in half. Tie tightly at the fold with additional yarn, then tie all the yarn strands together about 1½ inches below the fold to form the head. Divide the strands of yarn into 3 groups of 14 strands each and braid. Tie the braid at the tail end. Little eyes and a felt tongue add character to this little friend.

What fun to have a many-legged octopus to play with. Here again it can be done in one or many colors. The octopus requires 36 strands of yarn 5 feet long. Fold in half and tie at the center. Place a 2½ inch diameter styrofoam ball inside the head section, and cover with the yarn strands

Super snake.

before tying at the neck. An octopus generally has eight legs and this one is no different, however this is up to the maker, he may wish to have many more legs. Divide the yarn into eight groups of nine strands, and braid each of the eight groups and tie at the ends with yarn or ribbon. Felt features glued in place make this a most friendly looking creature.

A super-sized snake can be especially fun for any age child—to play with or just to have curled up nearby. It is made in very much the same way as the previous yarn snake, except that the strands are 25 feet long and the resulting snake measures about 8 feet. The entire snake will require six skeins of yarn (140 yards each) which may be the same color, or three different colors. For a three-colored snake cut 32 of the 25 foot strands in each color. Gather the three colors together and tie tightly with a small piece of yarn at the center. Form a head by using a ball of the left-over yarn of one color and place this at the center next to the tie. Spread the yarn strands over the yarn ball and tie tightly again just below the ball to form the head. Begin braiding the yarn strands using all the yarns of one color as a single strand. At the tail end tie the braid with a length of yarn and clip the yarn ends to shape the tail. Felt eyes and a tongue can be stitched or glued in place and he is ready to be snuggled.

A yarn bug is adorable and the perfect project to amuse a child on a rainy afternoon. Fluffy puffs of yarn make up the bug's body, and pipe cleaners are used for the bug's features. These little yarn puffs are such fun that the child may want to make many of them. The puffs are formed on two 3-inch circles of plastic, cut from a coffee can lid. Cut a 1½-inch hole in the center of each of the circles, then lay one on top of the other. Together the two circles are the puff loom. Cut lengths of yarn 5 to 6 feet long. Each puff will use three or four such lengths and the yarn may be all the same color or all different colors, just provide a selection and let the youngster decide as he goes along. Place the end of the first yarn between the two circles, and holding the circles together begin winding around the circles—down through the center and up over the outside edge. Continue around the circle adding new pieces of yarn as necessary. When this is finished, slide the loops apart in one place, and cut the outside of the loops, letting the end of the scissor slide between the plastic circles. When this is finished, slide a piece of yarn around between the plastic circles and pull tightly, then tie a knot. Slip the circles off and there is a soft yarn puff. Two of these tied together with pipe cleaner legs and tail become a bug. Tie more together for bigger animals. Just one is fun to have hiding in a pocket.

A yarn puff makes a good indoor ball. A paper bag with the bottom cut out could be tacked to the wall to serve as a basketball hoop for a puff basketball. A child can have such fun making and playing with these yarn creatures, the afternoon will be gone in no time.

The cotton ball turtle is very simple to make. The body

Yarn puff bug and cotton ball turtle.

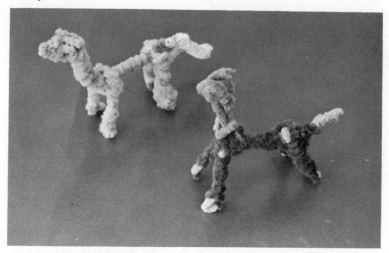

Pipe cleaner animals.

shape, head, legs and tail are cut from felt scraps and glued together. Then cotton balls are glued to the body to give the shape of the turtle's shell. The softness of the cotton just invites petting and its young owner is sure to oblige.

A package of colored pipe cleaners is bound to provide great entertainment for any child. Most any kind of animal can be created, real or imaginary, and it can be bent to perform all sorts of tricks and balancing acts. Maybe the young animal trainer will have his animals put on a show of amazing tricks.

A spooky spider can be great fun when suspended from the ceiling with a piece of elastic thread. A 2½-inch styrofoam ball is used for the body. Colored ones can be purchased or you can paint one if your child wants a colored one. Chenille sticks are cut into 3-inch lengths for legs and inserted into the styrofoam ball. Make eyes using tacks, felt, dried flowers or paper shapes and glue them in position. Tie the elastic string to a tack which can be glued in place on the spider's back. Hang in a spot where it will get a little breeze now and then—he's much more fun to look at when he moves a bit.

Spooky spider.

Such a fierce looking snake would delight a young child. Six wooden thread spools were painted and decorated with tempera paints. Felt eyes and tongue were glued onto the head spool. If wooden spools are not available, plastic ones can be decorated with colored tape or gummed paper. To assemble the snake string the head on a length of yarn and slide it to the middle, then tie the two ends of the yarn together near the head. String both ends of the yarn through the remaining five spools, allowing some space between the spools to allow the snake to bend. A crochet hook will help in pulling the yarn ends through the spools. Add a bead after the last spool, then knot the yarn ends together. The bead will keep the spools from slipping off the yarn knot. If this is to be a pull toy, an additional string or cord can be strung through the head spool and tied a short distance in front of the head with a long end for the child to hold. The string will be easier to hold onto if a bead or puff ball is added for a handle.

Spool snake.

Balloon animal.

Cardboard feet keep these two standing.

Pets Made with Balloons

Balloons are always a favorite with children. Maybe they would enjoy trying something a little different with their balloons. Two long balloons can be twisted together in the center to make a three-legged animal. With felt markers, paint the remaining end for the head.

Another way to use balloons is to add cardboard feet, which will keep the balloon standing up. The following diagram shows two patterns for cutting balloon feet. A slit is cut in the back, to hold the end of the balloon. Even if the balloon is tossed in the air to do tricks, it will always land on its feet.

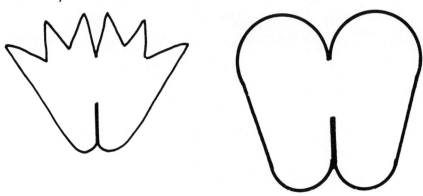

Feet patterns.

Rock Pets

Children find small stones and rocks irresistible. A pretty color, an unusual shape or an interesting texture will strike a youngster's fancy and in the pocket it goes. Perhaps your child would enjoy making some little pets out of his rock collection. By using tempera or acrylic paints he can add facial features or bright colored designs. He may

Rock pals.

The two rocks have been brightly painted, sprayed with lacquer and jiggly eyes added.

wish to glue some together or to glue on jiggly eyes. Spraying with a lacquer or fixative will help preserve the paint, and bring out the color of the rock.

Some felt or fabric trim can give additional character to a special rock. Here a spotted rock becomes a dinosaur and a lighter colored rock turns into a multi-legged monster.

Decorated rocks.

Seashell pets.

Pets Made with Seashells

Seashells are as collectable as rocks, and here some have been glued together to form little friends.

Nuts come in a variety of shapes and these also make interesting little creatures. Cotton, dried beans, macaroni, toothpicks and feathers can all be used in creating funny little friends. Small pieces of wood can be used to build on, or as a background for a friendly face of beans and macaroni.

Pinecone and Gourd Pets

Pinecones and dried gourds offer many possibilities for a child's imagination. The pinecone has felt paws and eyes with cotton hair added for a comical appearance. The dog's face was painted on using tempera paints and floppy felt ears added. This wistful dog head is perched on a construction paper collar to keep it from running away.

Nut creations.

Pinecone pal and gourd dog.

Felt Pets

Felt scraps and fake fur fabric are naturals for creating little pets. Here a spotted dog was constructed from a 3-inch square of felt. Roll the square to form a cylinder and glue or stitch together. Cut a rectangular piece for the ears, trim the corners and glue over the top of the cylinder. Spots, eyes and a mouth complete this little dog that can also serve as a finger puppet.

The little lamb was also made from fake fur fabric. Cut the following shape. Fold and glue A and B together, then glue C and D together. Fold down the two end flaps and glue in place. Stuff the body with cotton or tissue, small sections of popsicle sticks can be glued at the inside edges for the feet, if desired. Add eyes and little pink ears and a nose to complete this cuddly lamb.

Little felt pocket pals can be made in any shape. The round pocket pal is two circles with a little cotton stuffed

Finger puppet dog and fuzzy lamb.

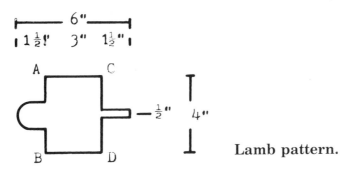

Lamb pattern.

inside. The circles are then stitched together, with an additional circle and star added on one side.

The little kitty shape had the eyes and mouth stitched on before the second kitty shape was put on the back. Some cotton was tucked inside before the last stitches were in place.

The puppy can be used as a little purse. It starts as a felt rectangle 8 inches by 3½ inches. One end is rounded for the face. Fold the bottom section upward on the fold line,

Pocket pals.

shown by the dotted lines in the diagram. Stitch together at the sides. Taking a little tuck at the bottom corners will give a little more fullness to the inside pocket. The upper section then can be folded down to form the flap. Felt facial details can be glued onto the flap. If desired, a nylon closure can be added under the flap.

A hand puppet can be fun for one child or a group of children. To make one similar to the dog puppet shown requires a piece of felt 16 inches by 8 inches. Fold and cut in the shape shown below. Make a cylinder from a piece of felt 4 inches by 4 inches and insert it into the neck opening. By cutting a number of small slits in the bottom of the cylinder it can be made to fit around the opening and then glued to the body section. Cut the ears in one piece to fit across the top of the head, about 5 inches long and 1½ inches wide and rounded at the corners. Glue on spots, eyes and any other features or decorations desired. Finally, glue the sides closed and insert a felt paw shape in each sleeve and

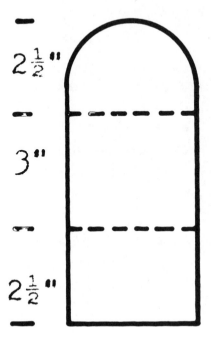

$2\frac{1}{2}$"

3"

$2\frac{1}{2}$"

Puppy pal pattern.

Felt hand puppet.

glue. After the glue has dried the dog puppet is ready to begin the show. Following these directions the puppet could be made to resemble most any type of animal.

Pets from Drawings

Every now and then a child does an animal drawing which is very special. Even though it may have been hanging in his room or on the refrigerator door for some time he

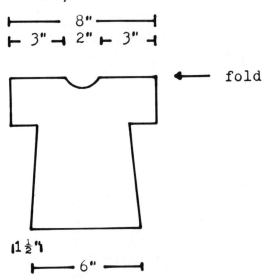

Dog puppet pattern.

Bean bags from favorite drawings.

just doesn't want to take it down. Maybe he would enjoy using his drawing to make a bean bag. Using his favorite drawing, cover it with another sheet of paper and tape it to a window so he can trace the drawing. Use the tracing as a pattern and cut out two of the animal shapes from felt. On one of them he can add the features, cut according to the traced pattern. These can be glued on, but it would be more permanent if an adult would machine stitch the features on. Then machine stitch all around the edges leaving the last several inches open to allow the bean bag to be filled with dried peas, beans or unpopped popcorn. After filling, stitch the last few inches closed. Now a favorite drawing can become a favorite toy.

Pet Plants

Part of the fun of having a pet is having someone to talk to—even if they just listen. Some people believe that plants

Pet plants.

respond to attention. With that in mind, perhaps a youngster would enjoy a pet plant. A bright colored Coleus, or maybe a little Impatiens which blooms nicely might be just what your child would like. There are always many kinds of seeds to be found in the kitchen which could be started; grapes, tomatoes, apples, oranges, lemons and avocado seeds all grow into good-sized plants. Of course the plant could be given a name, that would make it seem like a more personal friend than just another everyday plant.

Paper Maché Horse

What would be more fun for a child than to have his own horse to ride? Not everyone has facilities for keeping a real horse, but most everyone has space for this handsome steed.

A paper maché animal large enough for a youngster to sit on can provide many happy hours of play. A child will need the help of an adult to do this project. Please keep in mind that when working with wallpaper paste, clean up should be done outside, as this type of paste can clog drains. An extra pail of clear warm water for rinsing off your hands is a good idea. Try to make enough paste for one day's use, mix more if necessary, but don't try to keep any left over for the next day.

The body of the animal is constructed from three large-size oatmeal boxes taped together end to end. Several pieces of lath were taped onto the oatmeal boxes to provide added strength. Each leg requires three snack canisters—the narrow cylinders in which potato chips or pretzel rings or tortilla chips are packed. Stack the three canisters and tape together with masking tape. Attach to the oatmeal box body with masking tape, using small wads of newspaper to fill in around the top of the leg next to the body. Begin wrapping the body and legs with strips of newspaper dipped in the wallpaper paste. Glue on several layers then allow to dry for a day. Be sure to always allow the animal

Paper maché horse.

to dry after adding several layers. The horse will not be sturdy until all the layers have thoroughly dried, and it is best to allow it to dry as you go.

After the body and legs have been well covered, begin building the neck and the tail. Using two paper towel tubes for the neck base, attach to the body with masking tape. Additional wads of dry newspaper can be taped along side the neck to help hold it in place while the wet paper strips are applied. Continue adding layers, drying, and adding more layers until the horse begins to assume the desired size and shape. Entire sheets of newspaper can be dipped in the paste, then wadded up and used to pad areas to round out the horse's shape. An additional paper towel tube can be added for the head. Dry crumpled newspaper can be

This horse is beginning to take shape. The paper towel tube, for the head, is ready to be padded.

taped onto the tube for padding, then the layers of wet paper strips added to finish the head. Add ears and other desired features at this time.

After all the layers have been added, and well-dried, it can be painted with enamel in most any color with stripes or polka dots if desired. Add eyes, either painted or cut from felt, and possibly a yarn tail and mane—then it's ready to ride.

Your young rider may wish to make yarn reins, a saddle blanket, and even stirrups for his new horse. The stirrups can be made from 1-gallon milk carton handles, attached to rawhide boot laces. Plastic coffee can lids could also be cut in the shape of stirrups if the milk carton handles are not readily available.

Happy riding!

Index